# SCHIRMER'S LIBRARY
## OF MUSICAL CLASSICS

Vol. 2067

# WOLFGANG AMADEUS MOZART

# Sonata in G Major
## K. 301

## For Violin and Piano

2 Allegro con spirito
10 Allegro

### Edited by Henri Schradieck

ISBN 978-1-4234-2705-6

## G. SCHIRMER, Inc.

DISTRIBUTED BY
HAL•LEONARD®
CORPORATION
7777 W. BLUEMOUND RD. P.O. BOX 13819 MILWAUKEE, WI 53213

# Sonata in G Major
## K. 301

Edited by Henri Schradieck

Wolfgang Amadeus Mozart
(1756-1791)

Violin

SCHIRMER'S LIBRARY
OF MUSICAL CLASSICS

Vol. 2067

# WOLFGANG AMADEUS MOZART

# Sonata in G Major
## K. 301

## For Violin and Piano

4 Allegro con spirito
6 Allegro

Edited by Henri Schradieck

ISBN 978-1-4234-2705-6

## G. SCHIRMER, Inc.

DISTRIBUTED BY

HAL•LEONARD®
CORPORATION

7777 W. BLUEMOUND RD. P.O. BOX 13819 MILWAUKEE, WI 53213

# ABOUT THE SONATA

*Sonata in G Major, K. 301*
(alternatively K. 293a in the 1964 Köchel revision)

During a long journey of several months, Mozart composed six sonatas for violin and piano in the first half of 1778, of which the sonata K. 301 is one. It was composed in Mannheim in February of that year. In a letter from Munich, Mozart's locale before heading to Mannheim, he wrote to his father, "I send my sister herewith six duets for clavicembalo and violin by [Joseph] Schuster, which I have often played here. They are not bad. If I stay on I shall write six myself in the same style, as they are very popular here." (Sets of six were a common publishing practice of the period.) These six violin and keyboard sonatas were published in Paris, dedicated to a patroness, Maria Elizabeth, Electress of the Palatinate; this set is sometimes called the "Palatinate Sonatas." Musically they are influenced by Schuster's music for violin and keyboard in form and approach, graceful and spare, using the violin as accompaniment to keyboard in some stretches. But they also reflect the Mannheim style of pronounced expressiveness.

No longer a famous child prodigy, in 1778 Mozart was a young man of 22 trying to make his way into a professional musical life. Mozart's father, Leopold, had traveled with him throughout childhood, but was unable to leave Salzburg. Instead, Mozart's mother accompanied him on this journey, which began in September, 1777 in Munich. They traveled to Mannheim, an important musical center, arriving on October 30, 1777. Mannheim had an excellent orchestra and a court committed to music. The Mannheim orchestra was made famous by its radical dynamic effects, most notably pronounced dynamic contrasts and the "Mannheim Steamroller," a sustained crescendo of notable duration. Both Johann and Carl Stamitz led the ensemble, and composed music for its forces. In Mannheim Mozart met and fell in love with a young soprano, Aloysia Weber, who would ultimately spurn his advances. Mozart eventually married Aloysia's sister Constanze a few years later in Vienna. Leopold chastised Mozart for his amorous distractions and ordered him to Paris. He and his mother left Mannheim on March 14, 1778. Mozart's mother would not survive the final leg of this journey. She died in Paris on July 3 with Wolfgang at her side, far away from Leopold and their home in Salzburg.

# Sonata in G Major

## K. 301

Edited by Henri Schradieck

**Violin**

Wolfgang Amadeus Mozart
(1756-1791)

**Allegro con spirito**

## Violin

# Violin

# Violin